BY HIS SPIRIT

Pastor Bim Folayan

WESTBOW
PRESS®
A DIVISION OF THOMAS NELSON
& ZONDERVAN

Unless otherwise indicated, all Scripture quotations are
taken from the New King James Version of the Bible.

Keys for other Bible translations used in this book:
AMP – The Amplified Bible
ASV – American Standard Version
CEV – Contemporary English Version
GNT – Good News Translation
KJV – King James Version
NCV – New Century Version

NIV – New International Version
NLT – New Living Translation
TLB – The Living Bible

WestBow Press books may be ordered through
booksellers or by contacting:

WestBow Press
A Division of Thomas Nelson & Zondervan
1663 Liberty Drive
Bloomington, IN 47403
www.westbowpress.com
1 (866) 928-1240

ISBN: 978-1-5127-2741-8 (sc)
ISBN: 978-1-5127-2742-5 (e)

Library of Congress Control Number: 2016900960

Print information available on the last page.

WestBow Press rev. date: 03/08/2016

Table of Contents

DEDICATION

Dedicated to C3 Lighthouse;
A journey By His Spirit

Nevertheless I tell you the truth. It is to your advantage that I go away; for if I do not go away, the Helper will not come to you; but if I depart, I will send him to you.
John 16:7

He will glorify me because it is from me that he will receive what he will make known to you. [15] All that belongs to the Father is mine. That is why I said the Spirit will receive from me what he will make known to you.
John 16:14-15 (NIV)

That the sharing of your faith may become effective by the acknowledgment of every good is in you in Christ Jesus.
Philemon 1:6

'To be led of His Spirit is
To be fed of His Spirit
And
To be blessed By His Spirit is
To have been yielded to His Spirit.'

Bim Folayan
February 2014

Introduction

God is Spirit, and those who worship Him must
worship in spirit and truth
(John 4:24).

The Bible makes it clear that God is a Spirit.
If God is a Spirit, it then means that spiritual
realities can only be perceived BY THE
SPIRIT, which transcends human senses
(Romans 8:8). Ephesians 1:3 stipulate that
God has blessed us with every spiritual
blessing in heavenly places in Christ. This
then implies that those who have yielded
Lordship of their lives over to Christ are born
of Him. They consequently, have received
the power (ability) to become the children of
God. According to John 1:12-13 (KJV) *"But
as many as received him, **to them gave he
power** to become the sons of God, even <u>to</u>
<u>them that believe on his name</u>: 13 **Which
were born, not of blood, nor of the will
of the flesh, <u>nor of the will of man, but</u>***

of God." Due to this relationship, they have their spirits enabled to operate with God their Father. This enablement is what gives the spiritual consciousness (awareness). In 1 Corinthians 2:12, we read "*Now we have received, not the spirit of the world, but the spirit who is from God; that we might know the things that are freely given to us by God.*"

At creation, the Spirit of God did the formation of all things - "*In the beginning God created the heavens and the earth. ² The earth was without form, and void; and darkness was on the face of the deep. **And the Spirit of God was hovering** over the face of the waters.*" (Genesis 1:1-2). It is recorded for us in the Bible that God spoke to His people through those He anointed and the prophets who were able to discern when His Spirit speaks. David said in 2 Samuel 23:2-3 (NIV) "*The Spirit of the Lord spoke through me; his word was in my tongue. ³. The God of Israel spoke, the Rock of Israel said...*" God still speaks today and ministers By His (Holy) Spirit to His Children who relate with Him by the spirit. If we deny that God speaks to us today, we deny the unchanging nature of God. In any case, we see this manifestation in Acts 2:1-12.

God, By His Spirit ministers to those in relationship with Him, who listen to hear Him beyond their ears, even with their hearts. They know in their spirit/inner man and have the conviction/witness in their hearts that He is the One. They are endowed with discernment beyond the physical to spiritually receive and perceive what God is communicating. He speaks to them at any time. As they listen to Him and obey Him, they receive further inspiration, guidance, and are led in the path of righteousness, excellence, glory and dominion. The Spirit of God in them (Joel 2:28) gives them this advantage. *"...the mystery which has been hidden from ages and from generations, but now has been revealed to His saints"* (Colossians 1:26). The privilege of the New Birth (salvation) took place in our spirit, regenerated our spirit to have divine access, receive divine insight, knowledge, understanding and foresight on episodes in divine plans (Matthew 13:11). This is made possible by reason of the supernatural and higher life received through the redemptive power of Christ. Apostle Paul narrated to King

Agrippa, the enablement and empowerment received by the reason of divine regeneration. *"...to make you a minister and a witness both of the things which you have seen and of the **things which I will yet reveal to you**"* (Acts 26:16). When the Hand of the Lord is upon a man, he operates in the miraculous and the extra-ordinary. The Spirit of God and anointing did it for Saul (1 Samuel 10:1-11). This special empowerment is hinged on God's Spirit at work.

Anyone recreated and redeemed of God has His Spirit. He receives exposure (Psalm 119:130) to spiritually obscured things by divine revelation (light). God also speaks directly to his heart in audible voice as He did with Moses and with Saul. He does also through Scriptures as well as through visions and dreams as He did Joseph.

Christ has given us the Holy Spirit for our advantage (John 14:16-18). The early Christians at Antioch took advantage of this and witnessed the extra-ordinary.

"But the anointing which you have received from Him abides in you, and you do not need that

anyone teach you; but as the same anointing teaches you concerning all things, and is true, and is not a lie, and just as it has taught you, you will abide in Him." 1 John 2:27.

Chapter One

Spirit to spirit

"And I will pray the Father, and He will give you another Helper, that He may abide with you forever— [17] the Spirit of truth, whom the world cannot receive, because it neither sees Him nor knows Him; but you know Him, for He dwells with you and will be in you.

"John 14:16-17

The redemptive work of salvation awoke man to the Fatherhood of God; Achieved by the priceless sacrifice of Jesus so we may have life to the full as intended by God. Salvation ignited our spirits to God's Spirit. The gift of salvation redeems man from carnality to the nature of God (1 Corinthians 6:17).

A man's body houses his spirit. The real man is his spirit called the inner man. The spirit is what relate with God, for God is a

Spirit (John 4:24). A man's life flows from His spirit. The Bible uses the word heart and spirit interchangeably. Proverbs 4:23 says *"Keep your heart with all diligence; For out of it spring the issues of life."* A man's spirit is the citadel of his being, for Proverbs 25:28 tells us, "Whoever *has no rule over his own spirit is like a city broken down, without walls."* God's Word, By His Spirit is delivered to our hearts (Isaiah 59:21 NIV); we therefore must guard and fortify our hearts from corruption.

To truly be in relationship with God, it must be BY HIS SPIRIT. *"...those who worship Him must worship <u>in spirit</u> and truth"* (John 4:24). Those who relate to God in spirit and in truth receive development in their spirit to recognise God's ways and voice. *"My Sheep recognize my voice, and I know them, and they follow me"* – (John 10:27 TLB). A special ingredient is our faith. By faith we recognise God and distinguish His voice. We perceive His 'still small voice' (1 Kings 19:12) because we have received deposit of His nature in us by virtue of our divine and new birth. As we hear to do God's will, we circumvent ignorance and darkness (John 8:12).

Proverb 20:27 (Amp) *"The spirit of man is the candle [that factor in human personality which proceeds immediately from god] is the lamp of the LORD, searching all his innermost parts."* This experience grants spiritual sensitivity, discernment and revelation.

Paul in Ephesians 4:23 admonishes the Ephesian Church *"And be renewed in the spirit of your mind"*; for it is only when our spirits are pure and yielded to God's Spirit that we are able to receive divinely. Matthew 5:8 (Amp) says *"....especially conditioned by the revelation of His grace, regardless of outward conditions are the pure in heart, for they shall see God!"* When our hearts are pure, we are graced to perceive and receive (revelation, insight and knowledge) from God. David the son of Jesse was pure in heart all through his ordeal, trials and temptations and would not defile himself. He received knowledge based on revelation due to pureness of heart. A spirit yielded to God walks in line, in form and in tune with Him. God has given us all that pertains to life and Godliness (2 Peter 1:3-4) hence, we are equipped for His divine attributes for the higher and supernatural life. The Word of God and His Spirit have been made available to us for our advantage. Proverbs 6:22 *"When you roam, they will lead you; When you sleep, they will keep you; and when you awake, they will speak with you."* It is by doing the Word of God and operating as led by His Spirit in obedience to faith that we please God (Hebrews 11:6). Obedience demonstrate our fear (honour) of God. Psalm 25:14 *"The secret of the LORD is with those who fear Him, and He will show them His covenant."*

Relating with God as His children, the Bible points out in 2 Corinthians 5:7 that we walk by faith (The Spirit) and not by sight (the flesh/ physical things). There are several things that we cannot be physically handled or perceive by sight. This indicates the superiority of the spiritual over the physical. But thank God according to 1 John 4:13 *".....He has given us of His Spirit"* unlike those alienated from God, which the Bible described as *"having their understanding darkened.... because of the ignorance in them...."* (Ephesians 4:18).

The Children of God are enabled with diversified gifts. *"There are diversities of gifts, but the same Spirit. ⁵ There are differences of* *ministries, but the same Lord. ⁶ And there are diversities of activities, but it is the same God who works all in all. ⁷ But the manifestation of the Spirit is given to each one for the profit of all. ⁸ for to one is given **the word of wisdom through the Spirit, to another the word of knowledge through the same Spirit.** ⁹ to another faith by the same Spirit, to another the gifts of healings by the same Spirit, ¹⁰ to another the working of miracles, **to another prophecy, to another discerning of spirits, to another different kinds of tongues, to another the interpretation of tongues.** ¹¹ But one and the same Spirit works all these things, distributing to each one individually as He wills* (1 Corinthians 12:4-11). As we see, these gifts do not operate by human wisdom but by the will of God. The anointing by the Spirit of God brings the divine information and understanding that is beyond human wisdom and ability.

1 Corinthians 2:14-16 *"But the natural man does not receive the things of the Spirit of God, for they are foolishness to him; nor can he know them, because they are spiritually discerned. ¹⁵ But he who is spiritual judges all things, yet he himself is rightly judged by*

no one. [16] *For "who has known the mind of the Lord that he may instruct Him?" But we have the mind of Christ."* Romans 8:8-9 also lets us know that, *"...those who are in the flesh cannot please God. [9] But you are not in the flesh but in the Spirit, if indeed the Spirit of God dwells in you. Now if anyone does not have the Spirit of Christ, he is not His."*

2 Peter 1:4 refers to those of us who have been born of His Spirit as partakers of His divine nature (partakers of Divine experience). Since these ones are in sync with God (in Christ), operating His nature being His children (Romans 8:16), they are privileged with the character of His Spirit (Job 38:36). If we are of God's nature we therefore must not have difficulty discerning His voice but rather, to be sensitive and alert to His voice. God's Spirit is in us and always with us in the person of the Holy Spirit, which prompts us, teaches us all things and produces His abilities in us. In Hebrews 6:4 refers to those in God as those enlightened, privileged with heavenly gifts and as partakers of the Holy Spirit. We became immersed in Him, relating spirit to Spirit having received the power of the Holy Spirit (Act 1:8). By this, making us

the effulgence of His glory and power (His ability) in us. This spiritual ability is hinged upon sonship made possible by salvation through Christ. The Bible states in 1 John 4:17 that *"...as He is, so are we in this world."* By our relationship with God, we become enabled for divine privileges in knowledge and insight. This divine enablement and inherent ability stirred within us, aids our discernment of the mind of God. By divine enablement, we receive revelation of the Word such that it makes indelible impact in our spirits and lives. These abilities are gifts from God. Paul in 1 Corinthians 12:1 advises that we avoid ignorance in this regard. God in His generosity has bestowed us with spiritual abilities (John 3:34, Ephesians 1:3) so that we are equipped for the work. (Ephesians 4:12).

The divine connection that we have with God enables us to distinguish His voice (John 10:27). There are so many special blessings bestowed on us by reason of union with Christ and being joint-heirs with Him *"... has sealed us and given us the Spirit in our hearts as a guarantee"* (2 Corinthians 1:22).

For this reason, we benefit the deep things of the Spirit.

In order to keep our alertness to the Spirit of God, there are spiritual activities and exercises that are important to our new nature. The essential role of prayer for spiritual growth cannot be over-emphasised. Fellowship with God in prayers will keep us up with God's Spirit for full operation and other divine benefits (1 Corinthians 2:12-13). When we pray the Holy Spirit exposes us to the 'mind' of God. Regular communing and fellowship with God in prayer and study of the Word are both important in building us and in giving us the right depth spiritually. Since prayer is two-way communication, we therefore must be attuned in our spirits by being sensitive and alert to what God is also communicating to us whenever we relate with Him in prayers. As we do, we receive insights. Jeremiah 33:3 *"Call to Me, and I* ***will answer you****, and* ***show you*** *great and mighty things, which you do not know."* When we are in the spirit, by special awareness, we are able to perceive beyond the physical realm. Our faith-response to God stimulates prophecies for edification, exhortation and comfort (1 Corinthians 14:3).

We require alertness to God's Spirit (Mark 4:24 *"...to you who hear, more will be given"*). Being vigilant (Colossians 4:2), watchful and alert (Mark 13:37) to God makes us perceptive. Through prayer we get direction into God's Word (His will) expressed to us in the pages of the Bible. Prayers done this way are impactful. In Acts 10:4 we see Cornelius' prayers receive God's reaction "... ***Your prayers*** *and your alms have* ***come up for a memorial before God*****.**" Also in Acts 16:25-34 the Bible points out that Paul and Silas prayed and sang and there was divine manifestation. Since prayer is not one-way communication, perception and response to God's Spirit is only achievable when we are sensitive to God speaking, or His promptings (John 10:27).

1 Corinthians 6:17 say we are one spirit with Him. When the Spirit of God strengthens our heart towards a thing, it tends to serves as indication. As we listen to God in our spirit, follow and obey according to His Word, God's Spirit gets more inspired and the more

we will hear and receive through our spirit. Walking in God's direction leads us into His perfect will (Revelation 3:20). To effectively hear from God, it is imperative we are acquainted with His Word (the Scriptures) through study which presents us approved (2 Timothy 2:15). God's Word in 2 Corinthians 5:7 enjoin us to live by faith. As we maintain connection with God's Spirit, we must avoid every distraction. *"...let us lay aside every weight, and the sin which so easily ensnares us, and let us run **with endurance the race** that is set before us, ² looking unto Jesus, the author and finisher of our faith..."* (Hebrews 12:1-2). Anyone who hears from God without corresponding action grieves the Spirit of God.

The Word of God say in Romans 8:19 that *"...the earnest expectation of the creation eagerly waits for the revealing of the sons of God."* If we say are connection to God, it is expected that His manifestations are seen in us. Being our Father, and we as His Children (Galatians 4:6, Luke 11:13), His life, of necessity, must be seen in us. Reliance on God and obedience to His Word will keep us walking in this divine privilege.

James 1:18 (Amp) " *And it was of His own [free] will that He gave us birth [as sons] by [His] Word of Truth, so that we should be a kind of firstfruits of his creatures [a sample of what <u>He created to be consecrated to Himself</u>].*" Those born of God (John 1:13), peculiar in nature (1 Peter 2:9) are deified with this divine privileges and awareness. This spiritual consociate is what Peter described in Acts 11:12 -16 *"And the Spirit told me go with them, doubting nothing. Moreover these six brethren accompanied me, and we entered into the man's house: ¹³ And he told us how he had seen an angel standing in his house, who said to him, 'Send men to Joppa, and call for Simon, whose surname is Peter, ¹⁴ who will tell you words, by which you and all your household will be saved. ¹⁵ And as I began to speak, the Holy Spirit fell upon them, as on us at the beginning. ¹⁶ Then I remembered the word of the Lord, how He said, **'John indeed baptized with water, but ye shall be baptized with the Holy Spirit.'**"*

Our knowledge of God's Word boosts our understanding of God and the operation of The Spirit. This awareness facilitates discernment. Hebrews 4:12-13 *"For the word of God is living and powerful, and sharper than any two-edged sword, piercing even to the division of soul and spirit, and of the joints and marrow, and is a discerner of the thoughts and intents of the heart.* [13] *And there is no creature hidden from His sight, but all things are naked and open to the eyes of Him to whom we must give account."* Opening our spirits to God's Word engulfs us in the Spirit of His flow and because God is His Word (John 1:1), a yielded spirit to His Word picks up the transmission of His Spirit divinely. The Bible instructs us to study the Word (2 Timothy 2:15, Joshua 1:8, John 5:39). As we study the Word, we fellowship with the Lord. God cannot be separated from His Word. He ministers to us as we read His Word/ written Scriptures (2 Timothy 3:16) also He speaks directly to our spirits which always corresponds with His written Word.

I recall a dear lady once shared with me that she was upset with someone who then asked her a question to which she gave a harsh response. Few moments later she heard Words from Proverb 15:1 in her heart/spirit; *"A soft answer turns away wrath, but a harsh words stirs up anger."* Automatically she knew these were Words from God. For the reason that she is a child of God, and being a 'student' of the Word/Scripture, she said she instantly knew God was speaking. This is the outcome and the reaction of the Word stored in her heart coming active/coming alive (Hebrews 4:12). Perceptive of her to have realised God's voice. She became remorseful and made amends which brought peace to both parties. She attested that fellowship with God and acquaintance with His Word (Bible) enabled her recognition of God's interference. We receive direction as we accustom ourselves with the Word. God's Word as Hebrews 4:12 describes it, proved quick and active in this situation. God's Word can be transported and activated in our spirit in a flash but we must be sensitive and alert to it. Its impartation and impression in our hearts could either be mild or salient. Jeremiah 33:3 (NLT) refers to these revelations in our spirits as remarkable secrets.

Reading 1 Kings 14:1-6 we see that the Spirit of God reveals and instructs. *"...But Ahijah could not see, for his eyes were glazed by reason of his age.⁵ Now the Lord had said to Ahijah, "Here is the wife of Jeroboam,* *coming to ask you something about her son, for he is sick. <u>Thus and thus you shall say to her</u>; for it will be, when she comes in, that she will pretend to be another woman."* (1 King 14:4-5). We see that the Spirit of God, when we are open to Him also instils in us what to say (Isaiah 50:4).

Everyone who has a relationship with God must desire to be filled with God's Spirit in reflection of our extra-ordinary nature as God's Children. Each of God's children therefore must yearn to be spiritually perceptive (1 Corinthians 14:1) and this could be asked of God who is very willing (Luke 11:13). I remember that as far back as being a young Christian I desired **the fullness of God** (Ephesians 3:19). I recognised quite early that walking By The Spirit produces divine advantage and that it makes the Christian journey effective. Back then as a young Christian, I admired the Spirit in operation in older Christians. I would wonder on my role in the universal edification of the body of Christ (the Church). I cherished on my relationship with God and esteemed it. I gave His Word the ultimate place in my life. Little wonder now, I enjoy such fellowship with the

Spirit of God that it will amaze you to know that He is involved in my every decision. He has the ultimate say in my life and so I am duty-bound to honour and obey Him. Owing to this, He takes His place in me. *"Friendship with God is reserved for those who reverence him. With them alone he shares the secrets of his promise"* (*Psalms 25:14* TLB). I take precautions not to grieve His Spirit even when some things are seemingly justified. Rather than grieve Him, on one particular occasions, I simply negotiated His consideration, though taking into account that if He insist, His will takes prevalence. Isaiah 45:13 *"I have raised him up in righteousness, and I will direct all his ways..."* God is considerate, He presents His will in a subtle way. He brings His written Word to bear in your heart or gives you a nudge in your spirit, or He speaks to you in a whisper, at times it's laid in your spirit what to do or say with the 'burden' of it in your heart/spirit. John 16:13 *"However, when He, the Spirit of truth, Has come, he will **guide** you into all truth; for he will not speak on His own authority, but whatsoever he hears, **he will speak**; and **he will tell you things to come**. [14] He shall glorify Me, for He will take of what is Mine, and **declare it to you**."*

15

The Spirit of God promised that He will not leave the believer (the regenerated life/ soul) as orphans (John 14:18). He therefore ministers to his spirit and directs him in line with purpose. He never leaves the believer nor forsakes him (Hebrews 13:5). He is the believer's indwelling Teacher and Guide (John 14:26, John 16:13).

Fasting as spiritual exercise fine-tunes our spiritual perception. *"**As they ministered to the Lord and fasted, the Holy Spirit said**, "Now separate to Me Barnabas and Saul for the work to which I have called them." ³ Then, having fasted and prayed, and laid hands on them, they sent them away. ⁴ So, **being sent out by the Holy Spirit**, they went down to Seleucia, and from there they sailed to Cyprus"* (Acts 13:2-4). There are situations when the Spirit of God could compel us to embark on a fast as a form of separation or consecration, that arrest of our attention and concentration for spiritual benefit. Acts 13:2-4 account, portrays such transcendent benefit of fasting. By fasting, the Apostles were able to receive clear-cut instruction and direction in line with Isaiah 30:21 because their spirits were groomed, nurtured and trained for divine and excellent things. In essence, it was easy for them to perceive and comprehend the communication and the leading of the Spirit. Importantly also, they were committed to the leading of the Spirit.

Galatians 5:25 (NLT) *"Since we are living by the Spirit, let us follow the Spirit's leading in every part of our lives."* The Holy Spirit is faithful and committed to His promise to guide and lead us.

Many years ago, having just being brought into charismatic realization in Christ, as a young Christian, I imbibed full reliant on the Fatherhood of God and hinge on infallible life to those in Christ Jesus. I was to be married and I knew that the decision for the perfect date has to be through God. With about 52 Saturdays to choose from a calendar year, I knew I needed to depend on God for His ordained Saturday which my wedding was to take place. I was not going to choose just any date but one based on the premise of God's will. In prayer, I opened my spirit to God that He may lead and indeed He ministered a date! A date was clearly given in my spirit by God's Spirit. I knew that whatever day of the week it turns out to be, I knew that was it. Though convinced in my spirit, I lethargically still went for the calendar for the verdict of the particular day of the week my wedding date falls on. Lo and behold! It was a Saturday! Weddings are usually on Saturdays especially if you want good attendance. I was elated! I felt God's smile on my skin; I was lost in wonders of this awesome experience. I gained even more confidence and focused on working on this special date. Months in, months out, regardless of any odd, I focused. I kept the confidence and oh yes, it was a beautiful wedding, from my wedding gown to the hall decoration, to the crowd and everything about the entire day! It was indeed the day 'the Lord hath made'! (Psalm 118:24 KJV).

I depended on God and He ministered His Spirit to me, my thoughts could not prevail, neither any doubts nor confusion till His will was accomplished. I submitted to Him and I witnessed His reward

We see example of life By The Spirit in the early Christians in the Book of Acts of the Apostles translating to efficacy in their operation; they were supremely directed in line with divine purpose for effectiveness.

For spiritual growth, communion with the Holy Spirit is paramount. Earnest yearning for God and study of the Word also play essential part. John 5:39 enjoin us to search the Scriptures. Fasting offers us the spiritual augmentation and enhancement. In Daniel 9:3 we see Daniel abstain from food in order to fast. By this act of self-denial, we tame and subdue the flesh for the spirit. We must hunger for spiritual nourishment. *"...It is written, 'Man shall not live by bread alone, but by every word that proceeds from the mouth of God"* (Matthew 4:4). This statement was made by Jesus during His period of fasting. The Bible says His Words are spirit and they are life. *It is the Spirit who gives life; the flesh profits nothing. The words that I speak to you are spirit, and they are life.* (John 6:63). Feeding our spirits with God's Word enhances our alertness to God. When we feed our spirits with God's Word, we get nurtured and accustomed to God's ways, making us spiritually knowledgeable.

Getting our spirits in perpetual tune with God as well as enriching ourselves in His Word is how we obtain the divine sync, current and flow, the impartation and the unction. By these, we are aligned with God's will and purposes. Knowledge of His Word facilitate these reactions in our spirits. A constantly yielded spirit that is opened and submissive before God receives His flow and outpouring. Good depth in God's Word with compliance and obedience improves and develops this fellowship. We perceive His thoughts only when our spirit is united with Him in fellowship. Thus we enhance this bond through fellowship according to 1 Corinthians 1:9. For the more we are in His presence through fellowship, the more like Him we become as His presence is rubbed on us.

As His Word guides us and we obey, we enhance our ability to hear Him because we just don't hear Him and do nothing about it, but we must put what He instructs us to action. By this the inner man (the spirit is profited, Spirit to spirit, receiving life (The True life of God).

God's Word is received through our spirit/ heart (Nehemiah 2:12 *"...I told no one what my God had put **in my heart** to do at Jerusalem..."*). The heart/spirit, being the centre of our being, is what God relates with. This is where we receive and perceive the reality of God's counsel. Proverbs 20:27 refer to man's spirit as the lamp of the Lord. It is the place where divine information and counsel are shone/perceived or received. In Psalm 16:7, the psalmist says, *"I will bless the Lord who has given me counsel; My heart also instructs me..."*

As we invest time in fellowship, we learn of the Lord. Spending quality time in the presence of the Lord through personal fellowship and with other believers, studying and meditating on the Word, enhances and furnishes with power.

God's Words brings knowledge and power. His Words are His thoughts clothed with vocabulary to equip us in life. The study of God's Word exposes our spirits to His will and thoughts. His Word enlightens us and provide us with awareness to prevail in life. We immerse our spirits in The Word as we study and meditate or hear His word being ministered. God's life and His Word in us prepares and fine-tunes our spirit. It inundates our spirits for divine incentives. We recognise God's voice easily when we dip ourselves in His Word, in so doing we receive His leading and direction. The Bible assures us in John 14:26 that the Holy Spirit will teach and also remind of us of what God says to us as His children. *"But the Helper, the Holy Spirit, whom the Father will send in My name, He will teach you all things, and bring to your remembrance all things that I said to you"*. As we give ourselves wholly to the Word and obey God's Word, we enhance our ability to perceive God, His voice and His plan. Having and developing our understanding of the Holy Spirit, His nature and His operations, will all frame the believer for divine influence. Isaiah 55:6 says to *"Seek the LORD while He may be found, call upon Him while He is near."*

The Holy Spirit does not impose Himself or force His will. He permits freewill in order that we are involved and effectual in building our spirits. He is pure and gentle, He reveals, teaches provides guidance. He has emotion (can be grieved). He bears the presence of God. He is all-powerful (Omnipotent) and can be everywhere at the same time (Omniscient). He can be present with you 100% **at the same time** 100% with others. He is not limited; He has no limit and cannot be limited by anything. He is Almighty.

The Holy Spirit's present Himself available where believers gather in His name (Matthew 18:20). Fellowship and relation with fellow-believers (Proverbs 27:17) further boost our knowledge of the faith. In Hebrews 10:25, we are admonished about *"not forsaking the assembling of ourselves together, as is the manner of some."* The Lord commands blessings (Psalm 133:1-3) where His children are gathered. We see this happen in Acts 2:1-21 as the brethren operated in unity (Acts 2:42-47). They obtained the blessings in form of God's presence By His Spirit (Acts 2:1-4) as well as the manifestations of the gifts of the Holy Spirit (1 Corinthians 12:4-11).

To enjoy perfect fellowship and sync with God's Spirit, we must guide against disobedience to God's will which is a major deterrence. To be disobedient is to be of a carnal spirit, which the Bible says is enmity against God. Romans 8:6-7 *"For to be carnally minded is death, but to be spiritually minded is life and peace.⁷ Because the carnal mind is enmity against God; for it is not subject to the law of God, nor indeed can be."* Disobedience is quick to short-circuit the power of God in the life of a Christian. Relationship with God's Spirit is heightened by obedience to His will. Proverbs 3:5-6 enjoins us to *"Trust in the LORD with all your heart, and lean not on your own understanding; ⁶ In all your ways acknowledge Him, And He shall direct your paths."* Psalm 16:7 (TLB) referring to the Holy Spirit says, *"...He tells me what to do"*. Peter in Acts 5:32 mentioned that the Holy Spirit has been given to those **who obey Him**. Isaiah 11:3 says *"...He shall not judge by the sight of His eyes, nor decide by the hearing of His ears"*.

I recall someone telling me on how direction from the Holy Spirit saved her sister. She recounted that she had missed her sister's telephone calls and it was expected she gives her a call back, but to her amazement, she was prompted in her spirit not to. She found it odd but obeyed. It was later on that her sister mentioned that those calls were accidental. She had been eating out with her husband and friends being her birthday when armed bandits surrounded their table at a restaurant ridding them of all valuables. Having just received her dream phone as a birthday present from her husband she was bent on not disclosing it unconscious of threats at gun-point. The calls received by the sister had happened due to movement over her obscured touch-screen phone while she was been ransacked. She was grateful that her sister was led By The Spirit not to return her call, for if she had, it would have meant that the phone would ring to announce itself to the bandits, which would have meant terrible consequence from angered gang as well as the phone being taken. By this experience, both sisters including me who heard this story appreciated the benefit of having the Holy Spirit the more.

For God's Spirit to be effective in us, we must comply with Him. From the sisters' story, it did not 'add up' for her not to return her sister's call but she based her judgement on spiritual than physical perception. She did not base her reaction on what is naturally expected but on the leading of the Spirit (Isaiah 11:3).

By the privilege of sonship (1 John 3:2), we are raised as joint-heirs (Romans 8:17) with Christ, qualifying for a life of God's Spirit. The seed of everything that God is, came into our lives at the point of sonship together with Christ. This special position provides us the divine advantage. Referring to Jesus in 1 John 4:17, the Bible says "... *as He is, so are we in this world.*" We have been given the supernatural aptitude to be like Him. Galatians 3:27 reveal to us that we have put on Christ. The more we relate with the Holy Spirit and are responsive to Him, the more of His leading and reactions we attract. Christ's Word in Mark 4:25 does affirms this.

In 1 Samuel 10:6-7, Prophet Samuel, as obtained from the Lord said to Saul *"Then **the Spirit of the Lord will come upon you, and you will prophesy** with them and be turned into another man. 7 And let it be, when these signs come to you, **that you do as the occasion demands**; for God is with you".*

By acting on God's Word, we become well pleasing to Him (2 Corinthians 5:9). It pays to depend on God, to be determined in His will, being bold, strong and enthused to carry them out. John 14:16 (Amp) assure us of the Standby, the Helper - the Holy Spirit who will guide, teach and instruct us. We must develop in zeal and passion for God's will. *"Never lag in zeal and in earnest endeavour, be aglow and burning with the Spirit, serving the Lord"* (Romans 12:11 AMP). Coupled with a heart of obedience, God perfects operation of His spirit in those who walk by His truth, causing them to operate in His fullness, the kingdom of God functioning in their hearts (spirit). They operate by divine virtue and God's grace, all because of His fullness that dwells in them (John 1:16, Ephesians 3:19). Ecclesiastes 3:11 say He set eternity in their hearts.

In Ephesians 3:19 we read, *"to know the love of Christ which passes knowledge; that you may be filled with all the fullness of God"*. It is great blessing to be of the Spirit as recorded in 1 Corinthians 2:9-11 that *"...Eye has not seen, nor ear heard, nor have entered into the heart of man the things which **God*** *has prepared for those who love Him."* ¹⁰ *But* <u>*God has revealed them to us through His Spirit*</u>. *For the Spirit searches all things, yes, the deep things of God.* ¹¹ *For what man knows the things of a man except the spirit of the man which is in him? Even so no one knows the things of God except the Spirit of God.*

If we say the kingdom of God operates in our hearts, then we must operate in complete obedience and faith that does not wait for signs or sight (Proverbs 18:15 (NIV), 2 Corinthians 4:18). Obedience proves our love for God. By His Spirit, He reveals things to those who walk by His nature, those whose spirits are opened to Him. They are enabled into the deep and profound things of God. Their investment in the spirit produces a harvest of divinity. They therefore are spirit-led, hence they function in full and exact knowledge of God's perfect will. They are channelled in the right direction, in the path of glory and excellence because spiritual understanding is at work in them. We see this of David in Psalm 23 "***The Lord is my shepherd;*** *I shall not want* ² *He makes me to lie down in green pastures;* ***He leads me beside the still***

waters. *³ He restores my soul; He leads me in the paths of righteousness for His name's sake. ⁴ Yea, though I walk through the valley of the shadow of death, I will fear no evil; For You are with me; Your rod and Your staff, they comfort me. ⁵ You prepare a table before me in the presence of my enemies; you anoint my head with oil; my cup runs over. ⁶ Surely goodness and mercy shall follow me all the days of my life; and I will dwell in the house of the Lord forever"*. This is blessed assurance for those who make God their Shepherd and Stand-point. He leads them and to give them direction as they receive by His Spirit. We see from verses 3 and 5 that this leading by the Spirit of God provided David benefits and advantage. Paul in Acts 20:23 (NIV) said *"I only know that in every city the Holy Spirit warns me that prison and hardships are facing me."*

Our privileged position as children of God, earn us Jesus, *"...To you it has been given to know the mysteries of the kingdom of God, but to the rest it is given in parables, that 'Seeing they may not see, and hearing they may not understand.'"* (Luke 8:10)

Deuteronomy 29:29 says that *"The secret things belong to the Lord our God, but those things which are revealed belong to us and to our children forever, that we may do all the words of this law."*

God is a Spirit and he relates with our spirits. God's dealing with us transcends the physical senses. We are more effective through our spirits because God's influence. As we open our spirit to God, He provides us with the wisdom. *"But **ye have an unction from the Holy One**, and ye know all things"*. (1 John 2:20 KJV). This wisdom and intelligence is effective when our flesh does not get in the way. That is, we walk by faith and not by sight (2 Corinthians 5:7). God promises to give those who ask for wisdom (James 1:5). This wisdom is only effective when we live By The Spirit; When we are Spirit-ruled and not sense-ruled.

Opportunities and privileges that leads to success (Isaiah 48:17) arise when we are alert and sensitive to the Spirit. We receive prophecy or Word of knowledge (Word of the Spirit) described as fore-telling (which is a spiritual gift of insight) or by forth-telling (words made in declaration e.g. when you provoke blessings). Prophecy edifies the body of Christ, a gift promised ahead of times. Joel 2:28-29 *"And it shall come to pass afterward that I will pour out My Spirit on all flesh; your sons and your daughters shall prophesy, your old men shall dream dreams, your young men shall see visions. ²⁹ And also on My menservants and on My maidservants I will pour out My Spirit in those days."* Apostle Paul and many others before and beyond his days are fulfilment to this prophecy (Ephesians 3:3-5).

Daniel attributed this special empowerment or occurrence as access and ability given of God. *"Daniel answered and said: 'Blessed be the name of God forever and ever, **for wisdom and might are His**. 21 and He changes the times and the seasons; He removes kings and raises up kings; **He gives wisdom to the wise and knowledge to those who have understanding.** ²² **He reveals deep and secret things**; He knows what is in the darkness, and light dwells with Him. ²³ "I thank You and praise You, O God of my fathers; **You have given me wisdom** and might, and **have now made known to me***

what we asked of You, *for You have made known to us the king's demand."* (Daniel 2:20-23).

Peter in Acts 2:17 brings to light the fulfilment of the prophecy by Prophet Joel (Joel 2:28-29) concerning spiritual gift in the latter days. Prophecy comes by the Spirit of God and interpretation must be by His Spirit (2 Peter 1:19-21). This dispensation of grace has been bestowed on believers in Christ. By forth-telling we prophesy by faith (2 Corinthians 4:13) while in the case of fore-telling, is a product of revelation, spiritual insight and divine knowledge that is God-inspired. 2 Peter 1:21 *"for prophecy never came by the will of man, but holy men of God **spoke as they were moved by the Holy Spirit**".* The Word of God gave Ezekiel the ability (Ezekiel 37:1-14). The Word of God either written for us (The Scripture) or spoken to us By His Spirit is backed by the power required for its manifestation. We also receive the advantage of forth-telling. This is when in declaration we speak forth according to Divine inspiration, unction and the anointing of God's Spirit. By this, we speak the wisdom of God. *"In whom we have boldness and access with* *confidence through faith in Him"* (Ephesians 3:12). 1 Corinthians 2:16 say that we have the mind of Christ to align in sync with His will. In Isaiah 45:11 the Word of God says, "...and *concerning the work of My hands, you command me."* Glory to God! What an awesome privilege! This privilege we possessed by sonship (John 1:12, Acts 1:8), as kings and priests (Revelation 5:10, Ecclesiastes 8:4). The Bible in Job 22:28 say that *"You will also declare a thing, and it will be established for you; So light will shine on your ways."*

True fellowship with **sincerity of heart**, in holiness and righteousness attracts God's manifestations. We know of Mary the mother of Jesus that her purity and righteous living attracted on to her God's manifestation. When we are sincere with God by pure heart and faith, our genuineness will invite God's presence. John 14:23 *"Jesus answered and said to him, "If anyone loves Me, he will keep My word; and My Father will love him, and* ***We will come unto him, and make Our home with him"***. This privilege opens the believer to the association and participation with the Holy Spirit. It permits fellowship and relationship, nurturing and partnership made possible due to commitment and the special bond. John 15:15 *"No longer do I call you servants, for a servant does not know what his master is doing; but I have called you friends, for all things that I have heard from My Father I have made known to you"*. Those in relationship with the Father, He brings into His statures of being. By reason of their class/level and bond with Him, God gives them the enablement to know and to be aware of esoteric things by divine dexterity (Ephesians 1:3). *"And He said to them, "To you it has been given to know the mystery of the kingdom of God..."* (Mark 4:11). This special ability transcends the physical because of the indwelling power of the Holy Ghost in these believers (Acts 1:8). For this reason what they received and perceive of God is extraordinary and the supernatural.

Regular Fellowship with the Holy Spirit becomes necessary for the believer in order to be built up. We see this in Isaiah 50:4-5 *"...He awakens Me morning by morning, He awakens My ear to hear as the learned. ⁵ The Lord GOD has opened My ear; And **I was not rebellious**, nor did I turn away"*. The more we fellowship with God's Spirit, the more we are developed and empowered in relating with His Spirit. As we are obedient and not rebellious to His instructions and directions, God relates more with us By His Spirit. Also as we worship Him Spirit (John 4:23), prayer and fellowship, study and meditation we are promoted in divine dealings. God expects us to hear because He has provided us the ability (Ephesians 1:3, 1 John 2:27). The Bible enjoins us in Revelations 2:29 that *"He who has an ear, let him hear what the Spirit says to the churches"*.

God guides us through His Words and By His Spirit into His perfect will. He reveals things to us not just through visions and dreams but also by providing us wisdom and His truth which at times is delivered in a salient or subtle way to our spirits. The one who receives and believes is considered as blessed (Luke 1:45). Faith in God, reverence and love for Him, gift of discernment, coupled with obedience makes revelation beneficial. Discernment preserved Nehemiah and his good cause (Nehemiah 6:2-12). Sometimes things may not add up or may appear daunting but the effectiveness of it is in counting the on God, the One who revealed for a specific purpose. Remember His ways are not our ways (Isaiah 55:8).

God manifest His presence where He is truly welcome. His presence in such a place stirs His 'vessels' (His offsprings) with power, Word of wisdom, knowledge and revelation (Ephesians 3:3) as He provide them spiritual awareness. For the Bible states in John 7:38-39 *"He who believes in Me, as the Scripture has said, out of his heart will flow rivers of living water."* [39] *But this He spoke concerning the Spirit, whom those believing in Him would receive..."*

To walk in this privilege, we therefore must walk in His truth and light as He is in the light (1 John 1:7) in order to function in His state, His level and capacity. Galatians 5:16 enjoins us to <u>walk in the Spirit</u>, that if we do, we will not gratify the flesh and we will be able walk with God on to this privilege of His Spirit. Like Jeremiah, that we too may boldly say, *"Now <u>the Lord gave me knowledge of it</u>, and I know it; for <u>You showed me</u> their doings"* (Jeremiah 11:18). Submission to God's Spirit brings all these special opportunities and advantages.

"And suddenly there came a sound from heaven, as of a rushing mighty wind, and it filled the whole house where they were sitting. 3 Then there appeared to them divided tongues, as of fire, and one sat upon each of them. 4 And they were all filled with the Holy Spirit and began to speak with other tongues, as the Spirit gave them utterance". This was what the early Christians experienced, written for us in Acts 2:2-4. They were privileged to this experience, special opportunity and enablement because they heartily yearned for God. They desired for God's Spirit and they were filled. Even the Gentiles amongst them, whom they thought did not qualify, received, due to the state of their hearts which was opened to receiving the Spirit of God. They hungered after the Spirit and they were satisfied. *"While Peter was still speaking these words, the **Holy Spirit fell upon all those who heard the word**. ⁴⁵ And those of the circumcision who believed were astonished, as many as came with Peter, because the gift of the Holy Spirit had been poured out on the Gentiles also. ⁴⁶ For they heard them*

speak with tongues and magnify God. Then Peter answered, ⁴⁷ *"Can anyone forbid water, that these should not be baptized who have received the Holy Spirit just as we have?"* ⁴⁸ *And he commanded them to be baptized in the name of the Lord..."* (Acts 10:44-48). The state of their hearts, which was eager for God's Spirit opened them up to this special Holy Spirit encounter, which provided them the opportunity not just to be baptised in water but also especially to be baptised into God's Spirit. The Bible in 1 Corinthians 2:12 describes our unique consecration as such; *"**Now we have received**, not the spirit of the world, **but the Spirit who is from God,** <u>that we might know</u> the things <u>that have been freely given</u> to us by God."*

John writes to the Christians in 1 John 2:27 *"But the anointing which you have received from Him abides in you, and you do not need that anyone teach you; but as **the same anointing teaches you concerning all things**, and is true, and is not a lie, and just as it has taught you, you will abide in Him".* This anointing reveals and makes things known to us. It therefore becomes essential to maintain fellowship with God's

Spirit in order to maintain the connection. The Spirit of God brings God's glory –The splendour and beauty of His presence. Psalm 16:11 say *"... In His presence that there is fullness of joy"*. John said in Revelations 1:10 that he was 'in the Spirit', engrossed and overwhelmed By The Spirit and in His power, filled with prophetic insight; as to be insensible of outward things, fully taken-over by the spiritual and divinity. For Isaiah, his unique experience BY HIS SPIRIT made him boldly attest that: *"Everything has happened just as I said it would; **now I will announce what will happen next**"* (Isaiah 42:9 CEV).

In harnessing spiritual privileges, our corresponding action where required is essential (1 Peter 4:11). This is as long as we are certain that it is God's Spirit in operation, bearing in mind that whatever God's Spirit says or direct can never be at variance with His Holy Scriptures. Regardless how daunting, as we follow God's leading, we can be sure that He will lead and guide us through, till 'there is a way' (Isaiah 43:19 KJV).

As we give due diligence, being a hearer and a doer according to James 1:22 and an obedient follower of the leading of the Spirit step-by-step, we are promoted with even further access into divinity. John recount also in Revelations 4:1-2 *"After these things I looked, and behold, a door standing open in heaven. And the first voice which I heard was like a trumpet speaking with me, saying, "Come up here, and I will show you things which must take place after this." ² **Immediately I was in the Spirit***..."

This special opportunity produces advantage when mixed with confidence and obedience to the Spirit. This serves to benefits of us -the body of Christ (The Church). *"...and **where the Spirit of the Lord is present**, there is freedom".* (2 Corinthians 3:17 GNT). This freedom (advantage) to appropriate God's blessings. Acts 1:1-2 relate how Jesus physically operated with men while here on earth and how subsequently after His ascension He relates with His followers By His Spirit. *"...of all that Jesus began both to do and teach, ² until the day in which He was taken up, after **He through the Holy Spirit***

had given commandments to the apostles whom He had chosen.*"*

Up till today, His followers receive insights, directions, instructions, revelations and instructions just as the apostles by the inspiration of His Spirit. By His Spirit, He ministered to them, commanded and instructed them *"And being assembled together with them, He commanded them not to depart from Jerusalem,* **but to wait for the Promise of the Father,** *"which," He said, "you have heard from Me"* (Acts 1:4). This was for the Gift of the Holy Spirit for divine access and advantage as enabled **By His Spirit**. Acts 1:8 *"But* **you shall receive power** *when the* **Holy Spirit has come upon you**; *and you shall be witnesses to Me in Jerusalem, and in all Judea and Samaria, and to the end of the earth."* Power here is 'dunamis', a Greek word meaning dynamic ability, which includes divine perception, sensitivity and discernment amongst other spiritual ability and enablement. This power equips the body of Christ (The Church).

Being members of His body, (His bride), Christ was not going to leave us helpless or as orphans (John 14:18 Amp), nor forsake us (Hebrews 13:5). He said in John 14:16 (Amp) that *"And I will ask the Father, and He will give you **another** Helper (**Comforter**, Advocate, Intercessor—Counselor, Strengthener, Standby), to be with you forever."* This Comforter (His Spirit) referred to as The Holy Spirit is exactly like Him, He operating just like Him. The Holy Spirit became available to us when Christ departed physically from this world. He is omnipresent, being ever-present and available for the believers. As we saw in Acts 1-2, He is faithful to this promise. The availability of His Spirit to the believer means divine direction and guardian through life's journey.

The Word of God (Scripture) is wisdom. The Holy Spirit guards us into God's truth. He produces in us or directs us to Scriptures relevant and specific to our situation at a given time. 'Rhema' is Word of God for a particular person or situation at a particular time. It comes as the 'Now Word' (Word of the moment that is specific for a situation or circumstance). Such Word (Scripture passage) serves as treatment, solution or diagnosis bearing in mind what John 1:1 and

2 Timothy 3:16 says. Proverbs 4:22 tells us that The Word is life (reality, truth, precision, power) to those who find them. When the Word is received in our spirits, it comes with insight, prognosis and the power that brings it to pass (to materialisation/manifestation) as no Word of God is devoid of power (ability). Example is the account in 1 Kings 17:14-16. Even in our day, we witness the manifestation of God's Word spoken through the prophet of old (Joel). Acts 2:16-18 *"But this is what was spoken by the prophet Joel: ¹⁷ 'And **it shall come to pass** in the last days, says God, That I will pour out of My Spirit on all flesh; your sons and your daughters shall prophesy, your young men shall see visions, your old men shall dream dreams.¹⁸ And on My menservants and on My maidservants I will pour out My Spirit in those days; And they shall prophesy."* This is the privilege of the prophetic By His Spirit that we are now witnesses to that the prophetic is not limited to those specially called into the office but also to as many as are yielded to the Lord and enabled by Him on particular occasions. We see the messengers of Saul in 1 Samuel 19:20 enabled to operate in this regard. *"Then Saul sent messengers to take David. And when*

*they saw the group of prophets prophesying, and Samuel standing as leader over them, the Spirit of God came upon the messengers of Saul, **and they also prophesied**."*

Chapter Two

Operating in the Spiritual

"Your ears shall hear a word behind you, saying,
'This is the way, walk in it,' whenever you turn to
the right hand or whenever you turn to the left."
Isaiah 30:21

By faith we receive the Spirit of God as we
yield our lives to His Lordship. This Spirit
of God guides and teaches us (John 14:16-
18, 26). He is available to support and guide
believers in Christ. David referred to Him
as the ever-present help (Psalm 46:1 KJV).
In Acts 2:25, we read of David, a man after
God's heart say *"...'I foresaw the Lord always
before my face, for He is at my right hand,
that I may not be shaken...'"* It was by divine
insight that David saw. The Lord remains
the same, He is with the saints. The Bible in
Colossians 2:3, talking about Christ reveals
that *"In whom are hid all the treasures of*

wisdom and knowledge." The Spirit of God is the lead for our spirits. *"But he who is joined to the Lord is one spirit with Him"* (1 Corinthians 6:17). This makes us partakers of His life, wisdom, insight, special (divine) knowledge and revelation; hence by the Spirit of God, we live, we move and have our being (Acts 17:28). *"I will put My Spirit within you and cause you to walk in My statutes, and you will keep My judgments and do them."* (Ezekiel 36:27). When God's Spirit is in us we walk in His statutes, we are able to see, to do as well as align with His divine nature and character.

There are various gifts of operation of the Spirit. *"There are diversities of gifts, but the same Spirit. ⁵ There are differences of ministries, but the same Lord. ⁶ And there are diversities of activities, but it is the same God who works all in all.⁷ But the manifestation of the Spirit is given to each one for the profit of all: ⁸ for **to one is given the word of wisdom through the Spirit**, to another the word of knowledge through the same Spirit, ⁹ **to another faith by the same Spirit,** to another gifts of healings by the same Spirit, ¹⁰ to another the working of miracles, to another*

prophecy, *to another* ***discerning of spirits,*** *to another* ***different kinds of tongues,*** *to another the* ***interpretation of tongues****.* ¹¹ ***But one and the same Spirit works all these things, distributing to each one individually as He wills****.* ¹² *For as the body is one and has many members, but all the members of that one body, being many, are one body, so also is Christ.* (1 Corinthians 12:4-12). The manifestations of these gifts in building the church (the body of Christ) is very essential. The knowledge of God and understanding of His Word gives this advantage, enhances our ability, liberty, ability, insight, esoteric knowledge and discernment.

1 Corinthians 2:9-13 *"But as it is written: Eye has not seen, nor ear heard, nor have entered into the heart of man the things which God has prepared for those who love Him."* ¹⁰ *But God has revealed them to us through His Spirit. For the Spirit searches all things, yes, the deep things of God.* ¹¹ *For what man knows the things of a man except the spirit of the man which is in him? Even so no one knows the things of God except the Spirit of God.* ¹² *Now we have received, not the spirit*

of the world, but the Spirit who is from God, that we might know the things that have been freely given to us by God. [13] These things we also speak, not in words which man's wisdom teaches but which the Holy Spirit teaches, comparing spiritual things with spiritual."

These are demonstrations only brought about by relationship and intimacy with God. Paul admonishes the Christians in their relationship. *"So now, brethren, I commend you to God and to **the word of His grace**, which is able to build you up and give you an inheritance among all those who are sanctified"* (Acts 20:32). By being in relationship with God and by functioning in knowledge of Him we are brought into a certain spiritual reality.

A true child of God relates with God as Father, he knows when He speaks and honours His Words. When the Word of God comes to His spirit, He acknowledges and aligns with It. God's plan for us are good, the Bible says, to give us an expected end (Jeremiah 29:11 KJV). Since no Word of God is devoid of power, everything He communicates to us is for our ultimate advantage since He is our great Shepherd and Guide. To ignore His voice is to be spiritually and physically vulnerable. I remember a decision I once made out of seemly sheer logical sense. It seemed a rational decision but I got to realise it was one rashly made. I did not realise this until the Holy Spirit whispered it. The moment I got nudged on this issue, I realised I had taken things into my hand. It was clear to me that I needed to revert my hasty decision. I got it so clear in my spirit not to go ahead with my initial decision. Despite the hurdle that will be crossed to revert my decision, I was determined and grateful for divine guidance. I resolved to take steps, fully depending on God. At each step of the episode, I was expectant for divine instruction, attentive in listening, focused, determined and prepared for any consequence rather than to suffer regret for not trusting or obeying God. To my amazement the issue was resolved as if the situation I was correcting never existed in the first place! I felt ever so privileged to have a Guide, an ever-present Help (Psalm 46:1 KJV) and a Friend that indeed sticks closer than a brother (Proverbs 18:24).

God, By His Spirit related with Peter. **"The Spirit told me** *to have no hesitation about going with them..."* (Acts 11:12 NIV). This is Peter receiving instruction by the Spirit of God to visit Cornelius. Even till this day God communicates to our spirits in the same way. To those whose spirits have been made alive to God, they are able to receive insight and reality that amounts to divine advantage. We see Paul in Ephesians 3:3 testify of the way this has benefited him *"How that by revelation <u>he made known to me</u> the mystery."*

The believer in Christ is made alive to God. He has the assurance of the Father that he will not be left as orphans/helpless (John 14:18). This is the reason the Person of the Holy Spirit has been given to lead, to guide and to help us. The Bible says of the Holy Spirit that He will not speak of Himself but whatever the Father says or reveals. *"When the Spirit of truth comes, he will guide you into all truth. He will not speak on his own but will tell you what he has heard. He will tell you about the future"* (John 16:13 NLT). Note that the Bible says He shall tell us or He shall show us (KJV). In Psalm 23:3 David attests of being led in divine direction by the Spirit of God.

The written Word of God (the Scripture) is to guide us in keeping the right path through life. (Psalm 119:105). God's Word keeps our spirits alive to Him. We give room to the operation of the Spirit even when we do not fully understand it, for God cannot be wrong. John 8:12 "...*whoever follows me will never walk in darkness, but will have the light of life.*" Our focus must be that it ends ultimately in God's perfect will. Ability to distinguish this way is only possible through fellowship with God's Spirit for this is what produces the spiritual enlightenment (Ephesians 1:17). It is by this relationship that we truly know God. Therefore, as we fellowship with God through prayer, study of the Word and meditation, we trained and developed. By intimacy with God, we become more like Him in thoughts and reactions. The more we give Him free course, the more we are able appreciate His mode of operation. As we become God-conscious, we intuitively yield to God's Spirit. Romans 12:2 lets us know that by conforming with God and not the world, we will be able to prove (discern, determine) the good, acceptable and the perfect will of God. Walking with God in righteousness and holiness makes us fit and effective for His use. God channels His thoughts through us when we are yielded in spirit to Him. When His Word conditions our spirit, we become programmed in divine guidance. In Revelation 4:2, John the Apostle said, *"**Immediately** I was in the Spirit; and, behold, a throne was set in heaven, and One sat on the throne"*. Obedience to God's will and Word pilots us into God's perfect will for our lives. *"For who has known the mind of the Lord, that he may instruct Him? But **we have the mind of Christ**"* (1 Corinthians 2:16). For this reason, we must not struggle but walk in line with the mind of God. The more receptive and responsive we are to God's Spirit, the more open we will be to the dealings of The Spirit. Revelations 3:20 *"...if anyone hears my voice, and opens the door, I will come in to him, and dine with him, and he with Me."*

Even today, God still calls us by our name to draw our attention so He may address us. He is the Master-Communicator; He speaks to us by various means either through audible voice, inaudible voice i.e. to our spirits, through the Scriptures/His written Word, or even in songs. At times God can speak through interpretation of tongues or He speaks to us as individuals in the language we understand. Samuel as a young lad heard God's call. He prepared to hear God as Eli (his experienced master) guided him.

God as our Father provide us guidance (Hebrews 12:9). Any form of resistance to the Spirit of God grieves Holy Spirit *"And do not grieve the Holy Spirit of God [do not offend or vex or sadden Him], by Whom you were sealed (marked, branded as God's own, secured) for the day of redemption..."* (Ephesians 4:30 Amp). We therefore must give Him room because all things are made by Him and for His purpose; "For in Him all things consist" (Colossians 1:16-17). Those Born of His Spirit must recognise and acknowledge this when He communicates with them. They can discern His leading and are sensitive to divine occurrence because they have the mind of Christ as the Scripture points out (1 Corinthians 2:16).

"But you have an anointing from the Holy One, and you know all things" 1 John 2:20 (KJV). God's Children recognise His Word as it comes into their spirits and they are nurtured and guided by it. God's Word that we know and keep in our hearts guides us in His direction. So as we receive God's leading within us, it becomes easy to discern because His counsel and guidance are consistent with the Scriptures.

As we focus God's Word, His Spirit enables us to pick-up His thoughts. Paul said in Colossians 1:29 that *"To this end I also labour, striving **according to His working, which works in me** mightily."* God's Spirit in us serves as guarantee (2 Corinthians 1:22) and proof of His influence and action.

Keeping our hearts and mind pure preserves our spirits. Philippians 4:8 says, *"Finally, brethren, whatever things are true, whatever things are noble, whatever things are just, whatever things are pure, whatever things are lovely, whatever things are of good report, if there be any virtue and if there be anything praiseworthy - meditate on these things."* For out of a good tree comes good fruits. Jesus said in Matthew 7:17-18. We therefore must keep our minds renewed/purified (Romans 12:2 Amp) for the workings of His Spirit. Our spirits must be ready to function in response to the Holy Spirit, which Christ promised, for our assistance and advantage. What a privilege, we read in Proverbs 25:2 (KJV) that *"It is the glory of God to conceal a thing: but **the honour** of kings is to search out a matter"*. It is indeed of great honour to be insightful of what is concealed by God. Our relationship with the Father affords us the honour and privilege.

We are enabled in this divine access because of the Holy Spirit. His presence conveys the transcendent flow. The Bible says in Psalm 22:3 (KJV) that He inhabits the praises of 'His people'. When we praise and worship Him in spirit and in truth from our hearts, the presence of God is available and there is liberty of the spirit. Psalm 16:11 ***"You will show me the path of life**; In Your presence is fullness of joy; At **Your right hand are pleasures** for evermore."*

The benefit of the Spirit guided and assured Jeremiah on what to do. *"And Jeremiah said,*

*"**The word of the Lord came to me**, saying, ⁷ 'Behold, Hanamel the son of Shallum your uncle will come to you, saying, "Buy my field which is in Anathoth, for the right of redemption is yours to buy it."' ⁸ Then Hanamel my uncle's son came to me in the court of the prison **according to the word of the Lord**, and said to me, 'Please buy my field that is in Anathoth, which is in the country of Benjamin; for the right of inheritance is yours, and the redemption yours; buy it for yourself.' **Then I knew that this was the word of the Lord**. ⁹ **So I bought the field from Hanamel**..."* Instructions received By The Spirit provides guidance and assurance.

We see in1 Corinthians 12:4-12 that God does bestow His children with diverse spiritual gifts. The blessing of our union with Christ confers on us the inimitable nature that is in Christ. The Bible calls us joint-heirs (Romans 8:17) with Him. We are of God the Bible says in 1 John 4:4 and we are enabled by His Spirit since we are joined to Him as one spirit (1 Corinthians 6:17). Our relationship with God became Spirit to spirit. The Bible says in Acts 17:28 that *"for in him we live, and move, and have our being..."* In Philippians 2:13

(KJV) that *"for it is God which worketh in you both to will and to do of His good pleasure"* and in Colossians 1:27 that *"To them God willed to make known...Christ in you, the hope of glory."* Christ in us produces the ability to relate and operate By the Spirit. The fullness of Christ in us benefits the Church which we must edify according to Ephesians 4:12.

We can pray for revelation as Daniel did (Daniel Chapter two) and he received of God. This gave him advantage in his sector and within his larger community. As God's children, His Spirit is available for us at all times to depend on (John16:7 Amp). God's Spirit ministers to those who relate with Him and are influenced by His Word. *"The Lord GOD has given Me the tongue of the learned, that I should know how to speak a word in season to him who is weary. He awakens me morning by morning, **He awakens My ear to hear as the learned**."* Isaiah 50:4

"I will bless the LORD, who has given me counsel; My heart also instructs me in the night seasons." Psalm 16:7.

Jesus before his physical departure from the earth promised another Comforter, in form of the Holy Spirit (John 14:16) to abide with us everywhere, guiding and guarding us in the right direction. *"However, when He, the Spirit of truth, has come, He will guide you into all truth; for He will not speak on His own authority, but whatever He hears He will speak; and **He will tell you things to come**. ¹⁴ He will glorify Me, for He will take of what is Mine and **declare it to you"*** (John 16:13-14). Hence, we can depend on the Holy Spirit. With the Holy Spirit residing in us we are able to supernaturally receive, perceive and recognise divine initiatives (2 Corinthians 4:7). By Jesus' Word in Mark 4:24 *"...and to you who hear, more will be given"* makes us know that He expects us to be productive with what we perceive. Jesus indicated in Matthew 22:43 (NIV) that David spoke BY THE SPIRIT.

Paul admonished Timothy (1 Timothy 1:18) *"This charge I commit to you, son Timothy, **according to the prophecies previously made** concerning you, that by them you may wage the good warfare"*. Paul refers to prophecy once given of Timothy that by he be steered-on to profiting. Paul urges him to take cognisance and advantage of this divine opportunity. Paul in Ephesians 5:18 advises been filled with the Spirit, a state of deep infilling.

The ministry of the Holy Spirit is to enhance and support us. Colossians 1:26-27 says *"the mystery which has been hidden from ages and from generations, **but now has been revealed to His saints**. [27] To them God willed **to make known** what are the riches of the glory of this mystery..."* By this revelation we derive advantage. Prophecy edifies the church (the body of Christ) 1 Corinthians 14:4. As God's Word comes to our spirits or is revealed to us, our corresponding obedient action is required.

"Behold, the former things have come to pass, and new things I declare; Before they spring forth I tell you of them" (Isaiah 42:9); That is relationship! The moment we became God's Children (John 1:12-13), we become inundated with His divine life and ability. We belong to His class of being; those who are of Him, those He relates with and intimate!

Chapter Three

Desiring the Spiritual

"Call to Me, and I will answer you, and show you
great and mighty things, which you do not know."
Jeremiah 33:3

Paul prayed for the Ephesian Church
(Ephesians 1:18) that they will have divine
insight and deeper understanding. He prayed
that the eyes of their heart be enlightened
for spiritual revelation. We are not lost for
ideas or what to do when you have the
great Counsellor at work in us but we must
facilitate His influence by obedience and
diligence. Isaiah 30:21 *"Your ears shall hear
a word behind you, saying, 'This is the way,
walk in it,' whenever you turn to the right
hand or whenever you turn to the left."*

God guides us through our spirits. As we
abide in obedience and submission to His

Words, for instruction and direction, the more influence of the Spirit of God we attract and the more we are improved in communication with Him. Man shall not live by bread alone but by every word of God the Bible says in Matthew 4:4.

Spiritual gifts are to be desired. *"While we do not look at the things which are seen, but at the things which are not seen. For the things which are seen are temporary,* ***but the things which are not seen are eternal"*** (2 Corinthians 4:18). These gifts equip us and make us effective in the work of God for the benefit of the Church. Living by God's Word keeps us effective in the spirit. Effectiveness in the spirit produces the authentic Christian life. Christianity is not effective when it is not tuned to the Spirit. The Holy Spirit provides guidance to man's spirit (the inward/inner man -Ephesians 3:16). Our 'spiritual antenna' need to be tuned in readiness and sensitivity to the Spirit. When the 'mind of God' on any given situation is transmitted to our hearts (spirits), it requires our corresponding obedient action, which in turn translates to wisdom. Paul in Romans 7:22 says *"For I delight in the law of God* ***according to the***

inward man." The presence of God's Spirit (the Holy Spirit) enabled Apostle Paul's effectiveness on his spiritual journey, exploits and accomplishments (Daniel 11:32 *"...but the people who know their God shall be strong, and carry out great exploits*). Apostle Paul did great exploits simply because he was attuned to the Spirit of God. Moses understood the importance of God's manifestation. He said in Exodus 33:15 *"Then he said to Him, "If Your Presence does not go with us, do not bring us up from here."* Abraham was spiritually alert and sensitive enough to recognise and respond to the divine visitation that launched him into fulfilment of being the father of many nations (Gen 18:1-14).

Habitual faith response will help us in getting accustomed to the move and influence of the Spirit as well as enhance our hearing from God. We see Philip in Act 8:29-30 respond in earnest. *"Then the Spirit said to Philip, "Go near and overtake this chariot." [30] So Philip ran to him..."* His attitude to the Spirit was that of eagerness. Spiritual inclination is further enhanced by responsiveness to the Spirit. We get promoted in God by obedience to His instructions. God is faithful to direct us into His perfect will but we must resilient and determined, as God's direction will always produce advantage for us. He is ever faithful, revealing things to us (1 Corinthians 2:10) but we must give Him room to operate in us. As each of our spirits receive divine promptings and or signals, we possibly could tell. Paul's spirit was stirred as we see in the Scripture (Acts 17:16) but <u>more importantly</u> is **corresponding with the Spirit's leading**. If the Spirit says North, DO NOT go south! Avoid Jonah's regret!

A yielded spirit to God is filled with God's grace and power. Paul mentioned about the involvement (fellowship, association and communion) of the Holy Spirit in 2 Corinthians 13:14. The influence of the Holy Spirit is so important in the life of a Christian. Acts 1:8 (Amp) *"But you will receive power and ability when the Holy Spirit comes upon you...."* Jesus instructed His disciples to wait in Jerusalem until they receive the Holy Spirit, for this is what they required to be effective. Luke 24:49 *"Behold, I send the Promise of My Father upon you; but tarry in the city of Jerusalem until you are endued with power from on high."*

Extra-ordinary ability, divine access, information, guidance, insight, instructions and direction as well as divine secrets are opportunities open to us as God's children because of the Holy Spirit in us. Living in sync with the Spirit keeps our spirits awake to God and His purpose for our being.

We have this privilege through sonship. *"For as many as are led by the Spirit of God, these are sons of God. ^{15} For you did not receive the spirit of bondage again to fear, but you received the Spirit of adoption by whom we cry out, "Abba, Father."* (Romans 8:14-15). Being children of God and having received the Holy Spirit, we must recognise God's working in us and not give ourselves to rationalising spiritual instructions but to focus and walk in His wisdom. What we must know is that when we receive spiritual instructions, with such instruction comes the ability to accomplish what God wants us to do.

It is therefore important that as God's children, that we relate to Him in spirit for God is a Spirit (John 4:24). We also must be able to recognise His voice and His move, decipher and obey promptly. The only way we are able to do the great things/works mentioned in John 14:12 is By His Spirit as testified by the apostles in (2 Corinthians 3:5-6). Ezekiel did before dry bones could rise (Ezekiel 37:1-14). The more of God's Word that gets into your spirit the more effect It has in us when we act upon It. Galatians 4:6 *"...God has sent forth the Spirit of His Son into your hearts..."* Studying and meditating on God's Word assist us in divine insight. We must get habituated with God's Word because in seeking His Face, God speaks to our hearts/spirits. The Bible enjoins us in Proverbs 4:23 to guard our hearts/spirits. When our spirit is guarded, we preserve it from wrong infiltration and from the voice of a stranger (John 10:5). By discernment, as God's Children we recognise His voice. God speaks of good (Philippians 4:8).

As a follower of Christ we must desire spiritual progression. Apostle Paul did not settle for less. In Philippians 3:14 (KJV) He said, *"I press toward the mark for the prize of the high calling of God in Christ Jesus."* It is the will of the Father to grant us good gift –the gift of divine insight. James 1:17 states that *"Every good gift and every perfect gift is from above, and comes down from the Father of lights, with whom there is no variation or shadow of turning."*

The Bible refers to this esoteric knowledge bestowed on us in Romans 1:19 *"...**what may be known of God** is <u>manifest in them</u>, for **God has shown it to them**."* John 15:14-15 *"You are My friends if you do whatever I command you.* ¹⁵ *No longer do I call you servants, for a servant does not know what his master is doing; but I have called you friends, for all things that I heard from My Father **I have made known to you**."* Jesus, in John 15:5 says *"I am the vine, you are the branches..."* The branch is attached to the vine, so by reason of this connection, as 'branches', we are exposed to the mind and intentions of the Vine. For this reason, we have divine knowledge and speak divine wisdom. Isaiah 48:6 *"You have heard; See all this. And will you not **declare it? I have made you hear new things** from this time, even hidden things, and you did not know them."* Our union with the Vine (The Father) gives us this special access to hear, perceive, know and understand the mind of the Father. *"Now, therefore, you are no longer strangers and* *foreigners, but fellow citizens with the saints and **members of the household of God**, ²⁰ having **been built on the foundation of the** apostles and **prophets**, Jesus Christ Himself being the chief cornerstone"* (Ephesians 2:19).

In relating with God's Spirit we must work in honour of the Spirit. Reverence for God and diligence to His Word promotes this special privilege. *"Do not quench [subdue, or be unresponsive to the working and guidance of] the [Holy] Spirit. ²⁰ Do not scorn or reject gifts of prophecy or prophecies [spoken revelations—words of instruction or exhortation or warning]"*. (1 Thessalonians 5:19-20 Amp).

Some years ago, I was transferred to pastor a church in another town far away from where I lived. In the congregation was a lady gifted with prophecy. She would give specific words of knowledge and exhortation. Her gifting was outstanding and she was quite confident in this aspect of ministry. Respected for astounding precision, her humility and fear of God, she would declare fearlessly whether what she has to say will make immediate sense or not, whether it was difficult or simple to deliver and she will leave the hearers with impression that "this has nothing to do with me, anyway, I have delivered as the spirit of God enabled me". On one occasion she had a word of knowledge which had to do with me. She accosted me that faithful evening and in all simplicity said, "Pastor, you are going to write books and a lot of books." Again she emphasised, "Pastor, I am saying you will write and you will write several books." I guess she repeated herself to me because of my impassive disposition to her prophecy; which wasn't deliberate. Without despising prophecy and avoiding this as much as possible, I felt she got it wrong this time. I thought to myself - "But she was always quite precise." Confidently and respectfully she continued and went on to also mention about relationship with a respectable dear person that was going to go wrong. I thought to myself, "No way, where could she be getting this from?" In this vein, I mentioned to my husband with due respect to her and her calling/gifting that it seems estranged on this occasion. The facts were, first, I could not see myself being an author, it had never crossed my mind, neither had I ever given it a thought or consideration, it was not an interest, I had my hands already so full with ministry work, I had my full time job also very far from home, my children young and were not having enough of me as I knew the Lord would want it. I felt God knew better than to 'add to my plate'. Nevertheless, in honour of God's Word in 1 Thessalonians 5:19-20, I watched and waited to see how it would happen knowing that with God, nothing is impossible (Luke 1:37).

Years rolled by and I found myself inspired By His Spirit to write! Divinely inspired, I did not struggle at all to write, my life pattern and work schedule got re-ordered and fine-tuned to do exactly! God changed things! Within six months I wrote and self-published two books. As I completed the first two books, then the third, the fourth, then the fifth and still counting. By this inspiration, I have several manuscripts scribbled all at the same time ready to be developed into books. My relationship as mentioned with the respected dear person to me also came to manifestation, an uncomfortable process, but it launched me into the time for writing and other opportunities (Romans 8:28).

Never is our God an author of confusion; What the prophecy demanded then when it was given was prayer for insight and revelation.

....Who declares to man what his thought is, ...The Lord God of hosts is His name. (Amos 4:13).

The fact that we cannot comprehend what is revealed does not make it impossible or impracticable; for God's Word is living and powerful (Hebrews 4:12). When we pray, God listens and His response is delivered to our spirits so long as we keep in tune with Him. By this we are able to function effectively along the paths predestined for us as God's children. The Spirit of God gives us the wisdom and divine insight into mysteries and secrets for the right direction.

Prayer is an important action to take as our spirits pick up divine directives. By prayer we receive revelation, divine knowledge and insight so we do not walk in ignorance but in line with the Scriptures. Knowing God's Word enhances divine tuning and spiritual insight. *"...I have esteemed the words of his mouth more than my necessary food"* (Job 23:12 KJV). For Job, God's Word was foremost, the result of which was a secured relationship. Quality relationship with the Father is indispensable for spiritual effectiveness.

With great determination the Ethiopian eunuch studied the scripture (Acts 8:26-32). By divine intervention he was assisted. Psalm 119:130 states that *"The entrance of Your word gives light; it gives understanding to the simple."* To walk in divine knowledge is essential to our edification and that of the body of Christ (the church). Lack of knowledge means ignorance, which amounts to deprivation and devastation. God says in Hosea 4:6 that His people are destroyed for lack of knowledge. Knowledge brings awareness and information about truth. Knowledge is gained through insight and exposure to truth. A popular saying goes, 'Knowledge is Power.'

Some years back, I sensed a leading from God to start on a project to build and inspire women. I received divine knowledge for the task through openness and obedience to God's Spirit. I kept myself opened for direction and ensuring that I complied even with the challenging and daring aspects. I am proud today and grateful for what has so far been accomplished. David in Psalm 23:3 attested that God leads in the path of righteousness. My then seemingly ignorant pursuit has today translated into a notable Charity organisation that impacts homes and families around the world. It has been worthwhile and a great experience *"...for His Name sake"* (Psalm 23:3)

There are times when we do not fully understand where The Spirit is leading us on a matter but we must operate in His wisdom so we may end up in His perfect will. Paul and his team received divine knowledge not to preach in Asia and Bithynia at that time (Acts 16:6-7). Paul's team had the understanding, thus no misconception on the instruction. The same allayed apprehension in Peter considering that was unacceptable for him to have dealings with Gentiles. *"Then **the Spirit told me** to go with them, doubting nothing... And as I began to speak, the Holy Spirit fell upon them, as upon us at the beginning."* (Acts 11:12-15).

Operating by the leading of the omniscient God guarantees sure destination and destiny through Christ. By means of salvation available in Christ Jesus, we are enabled in the supernatural. The Bible tells us that Christ has broken down the middle wall of separation (Ephesians 2:14) therefore we gained direct access to divinity! Fellowship with God's Spirit increases us in knowledge and understanding of His will. This dismisses confusion. *"For You will light my lamp; The LORD my God will enlighten my darkness"* (Psalm 18:28).

Our position of advantage with Divinity opens us up to His ways and acts. Romans 8:1 states that *"There is therefore now no condemnation to those who are in Christ Jesus, **who do not walk according to the flesh, but according to the Spirit"**.* As we operate in response to God from our spirits, our minds and spirit get trained and developed.

Having been adopted as sons of God (Romans 8:15-16), the world awaits our manifestations (Romans 8:19 KJV). The Bible in 1 John 3:2 declares that NOW are we the sons of

God. Being God's, we are His ambassadors/ representatives (2 Corinthians 5:20) and therefore must stay connected to our Source. We are able to operate in special awareness because we are blessed with all spiritual blessings in heavenly places (Ephesians 1:3). This is for our benefit and that of the church –the body of Christ (Ephesians 4:12). By faith we receive insight, either deposited to our spirits or we hear audibly. We are able to hear God in our spirit since He dwells in us. John 14:17 *"...but you know Him, for He dwells with you and will be in you."* Since we are God's temples, we know that He dwells in us (1 Corinthians 3:16). Being in us, He communicates impressions to our spirits. *"... will pour out my spirit on you; I will make my words known to you."* (Proverbs 1:23).

On two different occasions, as prompted by the leading of the Spirit, I was to procure certain devices. On these two separate cases, I initially did not fully understand the need to do so. Due to closeness fellowship, I complied. On getting the devices, I did not fully appreciate nor comprehend their necessity but just to wonder, "why God?" Months later I was fully appreciative and thankful to God for the extra-ordinary benefits I derived from them. These initiative were due to persistent quite nudges and prompting within my spirit which proved to my advantage.

Abraham walked in obedience, in faith and in zealous devotion to God. This opened him to the privilege of an in-depth revelation knowledge of the ways, plans and purposes of God. A committed relationship with God brings revelation and promotion. The Bible in John 15:14-15 establishes that we are no longer servants but friends with the Lord. *"You are My friends if you do whatever I command you. ¹⁵ No longer do I call you servants, for a servant does not know what his master is doing; **but I have called you friends, for all things that I heard from My Father I have made known to you**."* It is this same qualification as the friend of God that Abraham acquired and he made the best of it. He walked in righteousness preserving his relationship with the Lord.

By God's spirit, we have access to divine secrets and truths. God's Spirit in us gives us this special advantage and awareness. *"who also made us **sufficient as ministers*** *of the new covenant, not of the letter but of the Spirit; for the letter kills, but the Spirit gives life*" (2 Corinthians 3:6). God's children, live in holiness, as God is holy. Cornelius' purity of heart got God's attention (Acts 10:1-6). God dwells in purity. His presence will abide where there is holiness and purity of heart (spirit). When God is worshipped in purity, His presence brings revelations, direction and enablement. God is willing for His children to have His manifested presence.

Anyone that truly seek God's presence we will find it. In John 16:24 the Bible says "*... ask, and you will receive, that your joy may be full*". God gives good things to His Children (Matthew 7:11) and He gives generously (James 1:5). He will not withhold from the one who ask. Jesus in Matthew 7:7 instructed His followers to ask and receive. The Bible attests to this in Matthew 7:8 that God is faithful towards our requests. God gives and man's role is to receive and receiving here is done by faith. We know that all good gifts are from God and He is faithful not to withhold it from His Children (James 1:17). As we see in the next verse (James 1:18), that His plan is for us to be His extra-ordinary breed, a type of His kind. Galatians 5:25 states, *"If we live in the Spirit, let us also walk in the Spirit."* God's design for these new breed is that we live the extra-ordinary life of the Spirit.

Our unique nature must be beneficial to the world we live in (1 Timothy 6:18). Our supernatural life has been made possible by the virtue of our 'New birth' in Christ (The Second Adam). We gave up the old and ordinary life taking up the new and extra-ordinary life made possible through Christ who has brought us into the kingdom of God's dear sons. By reason this Father-children intimacy, God speaks and relates with us. We hear God because we have His Spirit and we are His children (1 John 3:1-3). Jesus in John 6:63 says *"The words that I speak to you are spirit, and they are life."*

The Ephesians received the divine nature, ability and spiritual empowerment because they acted in earnest of the spirit. *"Then, when Paul laid his hands upon their heads, the Holy Spirit came on them, and they spoke in other languages and prophesied."* (Acts 19:6 TLB). They progressed to receiving the gift of the Spirit to prophesy. They spoke in special tongues (in unique languages; a unique gift of the Spirit). These gifts make us to operate in the fullness of God's Spirit, which releases supernatural abilities (Act 4:31-33).

As a young Christian many years ago, I wondered and desired how Christians hear from God. I was curious and interested at the same time. I knew God was able to speak to His Children but I wondered, how? I knew it would be by exclusive privilege and my curiosity was how to appropriate it. I knew I love God, that He loves me also and He listens to my prayer. He is alive and being a Spirit, He could only speak back to my spirit, so I listened. On a particular occasion I was in a meeting of young Christian professionals and as I worshipped and prayed, I realised I was hearing words meant for the group so clear and deep **from my heart** (spirit)! They were nothing I ever thought of, so what I was receiving in my spirit had nothing to do with my involvement. They message I got was not meant for me and was so profound, so felt obliged. I had the understanding that the fact that it was channelled through me didn't mean I should keep it. The words were edifying and encouraging, I should not deny the group. This motivated me to boldly; defeating my shyness, I DELIVERED by obligation the message meant for the group and did not deny them what the Spirit was saying to the group and this marked the beginning of my journey BY THE SPIRIT. *"And when they had prayed, the place where they were assembled together was shaken; and they were all filled with the Holy Spirit, and they spoke the word of God with boldness"* (Acts 4:31). I thank God for the necessity and obligation impressed on me to share openly right there in that crowd and for a very first time experience that served as catalyst.

In less than 10 years, I witnessed the manifestation of this maiden prophecy. God is truly faithful to His Word.

Chapter Four

In Spirit and in Truth

"But the manifestation of the Spirit is given to
each one for the profit *of all*"
1 Corinthians 12:7

The ordinary physical human life is not sufficient in dealing effectively and efficiently with the issues of this world system. In 2 Corinthians 4:4, the Bible refers to the devil as the god of this world system. His wickedness controls the forces of this world but those born of God will reign in life through Christ as kings and priests (Revelation 1:6), prevailing over Satan and his cohorts (Romans 5:17). This presents the supernatural and the higher kind of life given to those who have become God's children, whose old nature has been replaced with the new –Father's type of life (the character of divinity). They have the "God-life" – Zoë (Greek). Their human life has been supplanted by this extra-ordinary life. They are called the new breed because of their new nature. They are able to hear the Father (The Spirit) when He speaks to their spirits because they have their understanding enlightened. He lives in them (1 John 4:4) and they recognise His voice and they do **(obey)** His will (John 10:27).

Speaking of the Christians, Paul said *"So from now on we regard no one from a human point of view [according to worldly standards and values]* 2 Corinthians 5:16 (Amp). They have been born of God as His children, (John 1:12-13), the Bible calls them gods (Psalm 82:6, John 10:34), His heirs and legal representative (Romans 8:17, 2 Corinthians 5:20). They exhibit His divine nature, born of His flesh and of His bones (Ephesians 5:30). They possess the extra-ordinary and abundant life (1 John 4:4, 2 Peter 1:3-4) coupled with interminable and eternal life in Christ (John 3:16, John 10:10). They are special breed. They have His nature because they are born of God's Spirit. God relates with them as Children, they do His will and relate with God in spirit and in truth (John 4:24). They are equipped with diverse gifts for the perfecting of the saints, the work of the ministry and for edifying of the body of Christ (Ephesians 4:12 KJV).

"And He Himself gave some to be apostles, some prophets, some evangelists, and some pastors and teachers, ¹² for the equipping of the saints for the work of ministry, for the edifying of the body of Christ, ¹³ till we all come to the unity of the faith and of the knowledge of the Son of God, to a perfect man, to the measure of the stature of the fullness of Christ" (Ephesians 4:11-13). As we carry out and operate in these spiritual gifts, we are further developed. Our development spiritually benefits us and our world, (our sphere of contact) when we are obedient and in submission to the Holy Spirit who is our Guide (John 14:16 Amp). The Holy Spirit helps us to operate in sync with God and on to perfection. The Holy Spirit, our Helper (*parakletos*) of the same type, just like Jesus, helps the believer/God's child. He is with us believers in Christ Jesus as the Spirit of God. Being Spirit, He relates with our spirit to reveal things to us. He guides us in the will of the Father. He is our Advocate and High

Priest. Christ physically unseen but with us in Spirit.

*"For if you live according to the flesh you will die; but **if by the Spirit you put to death the deeds of the body, you will live.** ¹⁴* <u>**For as many as are led by the Spirit of God, these are sons of God.**</u> *¹⁵ For you did not receive the spirit of bondage again to fear, but **you received the Spirit of adoption by whom we cry out, "Abba, Father." ¹⁶ The Spirit Himself bears witness with our spirit that we are children of God"*** (Romans 8:13-16).

This preceding Scripture makes us partakers of the **same life** as Jesus. Self-control is very important so that we do not fulfil the lusts of the flesh by getting in God's way. The Bible say in Romans 8:13 that the flesh leads to death while the spirit leads to life. So we do not operate according to the flesh, we therefore must be attentive and submissive to divine guardians. *"The Spirit and your desires are enemies of each other. They are always fighting each other and keeping you from doing what you feel you should"* (Galatians 5:17 CEV). Based on what we read in this preceding verse, our spirits have to constantly be in dominion over the flesh. This is the only way to a quality life by the spirit.

In Acts chapter 10 and 11 we see how Apostle Peter walked in full submission to the Spirit in spite of the reservations he had. Ephesians 5:1(NIV) enjoins us to be followers (in spirit also) as God's true children. For if we say that He is our ever-present Help, then, we must give Him full room for operation in our lives and endeavours. By so doing, we walk in wisdom that only comes from being steadfast with the Lord. This is what procures us the edge in life. Deepening our relationship with the Lord puts the flesh at bay. As we love the Lord, operating in the Spirit and doing His bidding, we grow on to maturity and fullness in God's Spirit. *"But as for you, the anointing (the sacred appointment, the unction) which you received from Him abides [permanently] in you; [so] then you have no need that anyone should instruct you. But just as His anointing teaches you concerning everything and is true and is no falsehood, **so you must abide in (live in, never depart from) Him [being rooted in Him, knit to***

***Him]**, just as [His anointing] has taught you
[to do]*. (1 John 2:27)

The flesh cannot please God. Romans 8:7 says
that the carnal mind is enmity against God,
not conforming to God's way. 1 Corinthians
2:12-13 *"Now we have received, not the spirit
of the world, but **the Spirit who is from God**,
that we might **know the things that have
been freely given to us by God**.[13] These
things <u>we also</u> **speak, not in words which
man's wisdom teaches but which the
<u>Holy Spirit teaches</u>, <u>comparing spiritual
things with spiritual</u>**."* According to this
Scripture, the Holy Spirit provides us with
the special ability to also speak in special
tongues. The Amplified Bible states *"And we
are <u>setting these truths forth</u> **in words not
taught by human wisdom** but taught by
the [Holy] Spirit, <u>combining and interpreting
spiritual truths with spiritual language [**to
those who possess the Holy Spirit**</u>]."*

The Holy Spirit is the One that gives the
utterance (He frames the words which are
uttered). By this we speak the wisdom of God
in esoteric language. This is a language of the
Spirit, which is understood and decrypted

only by the spirit. This unique utterances ('tongues') edifies (boost, charges, ignites) our spirits in supernatural connection with divinity. *"<u>He who speaks in a [strange] tongue edifies and **improves** himself</u>, but he who prophesies [interpreting the divine will and purpose and teaching with inspiration] edifies and improves the church and promotes growth [in Christian wisdom, piety, holiness, and happiness]"* (1 Corinthians 14:4 Amp).

By this special ability we speak the wisdom of God in a mystery, even the hidden wisdom, which God ordained before the world for our glory, stating 1 Corinthians 2:7. As our spirit prays in this manner, we connect and relate better with the Spirit (1 Corinthians 14:14) and our communication is more effective. In this process we receive the spiritual insight, deeper understanding, exclusive and esoteric knowledge on things or specific direction and information by God's Spirit (Psalm 32:8). It is great honour and privilege to know what God is doing! The information we receive helps us, guides us and comforts us. This is the role of our Counsellor and Comforter. *For He Himself has said, "I will never leave you nor forsake you.'* **6** *So we may boldly say:*

"The Lord is my helper; I will not fear." It is important therefore that we know and serve Him IN SPIRIT and IN TRUTH (John 4:23).

Cornelius and His household received the Holy Spirit as Peter spoke. *"While Peter was still speaking these words, the Holy Spirit fell upon all those who heard the word. ⁴⁵ And those of the circumcision who believed were astonished, as many as came with Peter, because the gift of the Holy Spirit had been poured out on the Gentiles also."* Their spirits were submissive and yearned for God, so they RECEIVED!

We are strengthened in spirit (in our inner man/spirit man) through regular fellowship/ prayers (communion/relationship) with God. Jesus often slipped away from the crowd to be alone **so He could pray** (Luke 5:16 NCV). He esteemed His fellowship time with the Father above all. Prayers guided Him; for by it He received directions and instructions, by it He received strength. He once returned from prayer and announced that it was time to move to another city (Mark 1:38) and another time of prayer resulted in the selection of His disciples (Luke 6:12-13). Jesus says He does things the way He is told of the Father (John 5:30 AMP). As a result of prayers, He was ready for the persecution, tribulation and crucifixion that awaited Him.

In Isaiah 42:9 the Bible states that *"Behold, the former things have come to pass, and new things I declare; Before they spring forth I tell you of them."* We need to be sensitive and alert as well as responsive to God to access the benefit of His revelation and secret things or plans. Responsiveness to the Holy Spirit improves us in this special gift. Psalm 25:14 (TLB) says, *"Friendship with God is <u>reserved for those who reverence</u> him. With them alone he shares the secrets of His promises."* They recognise His dealings and don't compromise His instructions. They revere Him and recognise His Spirit is present in a place. They can ascertain when His Spirit is in operation.

They recognise that when anything is of God, it carries His presence and distinction. Their focus, intimacy, fellowship and communication with the Spirit of God attribute to this. John 10:3-4 *"To him the doorkeeper opens, and the sheep hear his* *voice; and he calls his own sheep by name and leads them out. ⁴ And when he brings out his own sheep, he goes before them; and <u>the sheep follow him, for they know his voice</u>.*" They do not walk in darkness; they understand Him and His way because they follow His trend obediently. They seek for His will to be done, fervent in pleasing Him by their actions and responses to divine order of things. They honour Him by performing His Word, and doing what He says regardless, even when the details are not yet clear to physical senses. They are the ones referred to in Hebrews 5:14 *"...those who **by reason of use** have their senses exercised to discern...."* They are the ones who simply just act in accordance to His Word and His leading. They are the expression of His will and Word. They know that the more 'into Him' they are, the more 'into them' He is. They are sensitive and reactive to His Spirit. They act in faith, understanding that their faith moves God, that by their trust and confidence in Him, they develop a relationship of mutual trust. Since they believe God, they are able to see and hear by Faith. John 11:40 *"Jesus said to her, "Did I not say to you that if you would believe you would see the glory of God?"*

These are the ones able to see and hear through their spirit (BY HIS SPIRIT) because their spirits are sensitive to God hence their spiritual eyes and ears are developed. The book of Jude enjoins us to develop ourselves in this manner stating in Jude 1:20 *"But you, beloved, building yourselves up on your most holy faith, praying in the Holy Spirit"*.

Abraham was sensitive to God that God shared 'secret and deep' things with him and called Him friend. By this friendship/closeness, God revealed/informed and involved Abraham in what He planned against Sodom and Gomorrah. What a privilege position for Abraham, that saved his nephew Lot! (Genesis 18:16-22).

Our eyes must not be blurred neither our ears dull to spiritual things. God at times communicates to us through situations and events, but more importantly is our sensitivity, alertness and strict obedience to His Spirit which amounts in discernment and divine results. We cannot afford to compromise, if we say we desire spiritual upliftment. By spiritual wisdom and understanding, we pick-up what God is communicating through situations. *"While **Peter thought** on the vision, **the Spirit said** to him, 'Behold, three men seeking you'"* (Acts 10:19).

God's ministers (those who serve and relate with His Spirit) receives information from the Spirit on behalf of someone and at times, He speaks to both. 1 Corinthians 2:7-10 (KJV), in verse 10 it states: *"But God hath revealed them unto us **<u>BY HIS SPIRIT</u>**: for the Spirit searcheth all things, yea, the deep things of God."* Besides, God, the Master-communicator communicates through any means that has His influence. 2 Corinthians 3:5-6 states that *"Not that we are sufficient of ourselves to think of anything as being from ourselves, but our sufficiency is from God, ⁶ **who also made us sufficient** as ministers of the new covenant, not of the letter <u>but of the Spirit</u>; for the letter kills, but the Spirit gives life."* The apostles state in 2 Corinthians 4:7 (TLB) says *"...Everyone can see that the glorious power within must be from God and is not our own."*

With Timothy's interest at heart, Paul stirred and charged him in 1 Timothy 1:18 *"This charge I commit to you, son Timothy, according to the prophecies previously made concerning you, that by them you may wage the good warfare."* Paul here is stimulating Timothy to crave and 'fight' (be determined) for the things of the Spirit. Just as 1 Thessalonians 5:19-21 advises that we *"Do not quench the Spirit; do not despise prophecies. Test all things; hold fast what is good."* Meaning we should aspire and promote spiritual things which is the only way to bear or continue to bear the nine fruits of the spirit listed in Galatians 5:22-23 (NLT) - *"But the Holy Spirit produces this kind of fruit in our lives: love, joy, peace, patience, kindness, goodness, faithfulness, [23] gentleness, and self-control..."* In this vain, we therefore must invest in the spiritual by relation, interaction and response to the Spirit.

Investing in the things of the Spirit involves conscious self-sacrifices and stringent obedience. The Holy Spirit will work and minister through those who avail themselves and are truly dedicated. He knows all things and He is not deceived. It is advisable to give Him first-place in our hearts that He may be able to do His will and have His ways in us. It then implies that we give Him room and not restrict His ways in us. As He operates in us, our submission to His will is always be to our benefit.

He is our ever-present to Help. The great Shepherd with great and perfect plan for us. He has got excellent plans for us in order for a glorious future. For the purpose-driven Christian, living a life of the spirit and bearing fruits is essential. The more we are yielded in our walk with God and are submissive to His Spirit, the more we receive insights and wisdom that puts us over in life; and the better get in relating with Him. Likewise, the more alert and yielded to His spirit we are, the more we are able hear Him and receive from Him. In essence, our spiritual antennae and reception are developed.

Obedience to God's Spirit is a key factor for attracting God's influence around us. Walking with God will require taking God-inspired actions. The unction and the jolt we experience in our spirit implies corresponding reaction in order for the achievement of divine counsel. He is our Counsellor, our Great High Priest (Isaiah 9:6).

Hebrews 13:20-21

*"Now may the God of peace who brought up our Lord Jesus from the dead, that great Shepherd of the sheep, through the blood of the everlasting covenant, ²¹ **make you complete** in every good work to do His will, **working in you** what is well pleasing in His sight, through Jesus Christ, to whom be glory forever and ever. Amen."*

Conclusion

*"Which in other ages was not made known to the
sons of men, as <u>it has now been revealed</u> by the
Spirit to His holy apostles and prophets"*
Ephesians 3:5

Christ offered the salvation that brought
us back to God. He communicates with
us today through the ministry of the Holy
Spirit, enabling us to know the heart of the
Father. In recent times, prophecy became a
more regular feature in churches of many
different denominations compared with
many centuries ago when prophecy was
almost unknown. A distinctive feature of
prophecies these days is that it comes not
only from well-known prophets but also from
the average believing Christians, fulfilling
Joel 2:28. However, there are inevitable
cases of false prophecies by the wrong people
compounded by lack of widespread teaching
on prophecy by the church where people are

trained and receive learning on how to listen and hear God before sharing with others. David in Psalm 45:1 (KJV) could say that his heart was inditing a good matter. This is only because the Spirit of God had revealed something great or said something special to his heart. He mentioned in Psalm 16:7 that *"I will bless the Lord who has given me counsel;* ***My heart also instructs me*** *in the night seasons."*

Prophecies can carefully be weighed and tested. Apostle Paul warned the Thessalonian church that prophecies should not be treated with contempt, but tested; holding on to good while avoiding every kind of evil (1 Thessalonians 5:19-22).

Salvation offers the regeneration that brings new life (Colossians 3:10) with quickening spirit (1 Corinthians 15:45) -a life-giving Spirit. Christ is the power in this new and supernatural life that we live. He is the life we live and our lives are encapsulated in Him (Colossians 3:3). Our ordinary life has been supplanted by inimitable life, which is from above (of the Father; Divine). As Christ is received as Lord over our lives, He becomes our wisdom. The Bible points out in Colossians 2:3 that in Christ are hid all the treasures of wisdom and knowledge. These include the knowledge and understanding of all learning, insight into reality, divine ability to see with the eyes and the mind of God (in us), thereby seeing, perceiving and understanding things from His own perspective.

As we walk in the light (revelation) of the spiritual, as God is in the light (1 John 1:17), we are promoted (transformed) from glory to glory (2 Corinthians 3:18) in His wisdom and knowledge (Ephesians 1:17-18).

God's Word is wisdom, and the Spirit of God brings understanding and revelation (Isaiah 11:2-3). God's Word benefits us when received with understanding. The influence of God's Spirit is quite essential for real Christian living. Proverbs 29:18 lets us know that where there is no revelation, people cast off restraints (KJV says the people perish). When we have Christ in our lives, His wisdom is deposited into our spirit (1 Corinthians 1:30), which gives us the advantage in life. This wisdom helped Nehemiah to prevail over the plot of his adversaries. ***"Then I perceived*** *that God had not sent him at all, but that he pronounced this prophecy against me because Tobiah and Sanballat had hired him. ^{13} For this reason he was hired, that I should be afraid and act that way and sin, so that they might have cause for an evil report, that they might reproach me"* (Nehemiah 6:12-13). This wisdom delivered Nehemiah.

When Jesus asked His disciples in Matthew 16:15-17 "Who do you say that I am?" Peter answered and said, "You are Christ, the Son of the living God." Jesus' response was "Blessed are you, Simon Bar-Jonah, for flesh and blood has not revealed this to you, but My Father who is in heaven." Peter could only know Him by revelation.

The believers in Christ are a type of this special breed; a kind of first fruits (a sample of what He created to be consecrated to Himself); What 1 Peter 2:9 call the chosen race, God's own purchased, special people, set forth for wonderful deeds and for <u>display of the virtues</u> and perfections (reflection) of Him.

Let us therefore not live by the flesh but BY THE SPIRIT.

Prayer

Dear Heavenly Father, I yield my spirit to You that You may have Your way in me at all times and keep me sensitive to Your Spirit; That I may be a true reflection of Your glory and virtues, in Jesus Name I pray (Amen).

'To be led of the Spirit is to
be fed of the Spirit
and to be fed of His Spirit is
to be led of His Spirit'
-Be led!

For the spirit leads to life
and the flesh to death!
(John 6:63, Romans 8:4-9, Galatians 6:8).

*"For as many as **are led** by the Spirit
of God, **they are** the sons of God."*
-Romans 8:14 (KJV)

Are you?

Printed in the United States
By Bookmasters